~A BINGO BOOK~

Maryland
Bingo Book

COMPLETE BINGO GAME IN A BOOK

Written By Rebecca Stark

ISBN 978-0-87386-513-5

Educational Books 'n' Bingo

Printed in the U.S.A.

DIRECTIONS

INCLUDED:

List of Terms

Templates for Additional Terms and Clues

2 Clues per Term

30 Unique Bingo Cards

Markers

1. **Either cut apart the book or make copies of ALL the sheets. You might want to make an extra copy of the clue sheets to use for introduction and review. Keep the sheets in an envelope for easy reuse.**

2. Cut apart the call cards with terms and clues.

3. Pass out one bingo card per student. There are enough for a class of 30.

4. Pass out markers. You may cut apart the markers included in this book or use any other small items of your choice.

5. Decide whether or not you will require the entire card to be filled. Requiring the entire card to be filled provides a better review. However, if you have a short time to fill, you may prefer to have them do the just the border or some other format. Tell the class before you begin what is required.

6. There are 50 terms. Read the list before you begin. If there are any terms that have not been covered in class, you may want to read to the students the term and clues before you begin.

7. There is a blank space in the middle of each card. You can instruct the students to use it as a free space or you can write in answers to cover terms not included. Of course, in this case you would create your own clues. (Templates provided.)

8. Shuffle the cards and place them in a pile. Two or three clues are provided for each term. If you plan to play the game with the same group more than once, you might want to choose a different clue for each game. If not, you may choose to use more than one clue.

9. Be sure to keep the cards you have used for the present game in a separate pile. When a student calls, "Bingo," he or she will have to verify that the correct answers are on his or her card AND that the markers were placed in response to the proper questions. Pull out the cards that are on the student's card keeping them in the order they were used in the game. Read each clue as it was given and ask the student to identify the correct answer from his or her card.

10. If the student has the correct answers on the card AND has shown that they were marked in response to the *correct questions,* then that student is the winner and the game is over. If the student does not have the correct answers on the card OR he or she marked the answers in response to *the wrong questions,* then the game continues until there is a proper winner.

11. If you want to play again, reshuffle the cards and begin again.

Have fun!

TERMS INCLUDED

Annapolis	Flag
Antietam	Fossil(s)
Atlantic Coastal Plain	Frederick
Backbone Mountain	Industry (-ies)
Baltimore	Judicial Branch
Baltimore Oriole	Legislative Branch
Benjamin Banneker	Livestock
Bethesda	Mid-Atlantic
Black-Eyed Susan	Piedmont
Blue Crab(s)	Plateau
Blue Ridge	Province of Maryland
Border States	Ridge and Valley
Border(s)	River(s)
Cabinet	George Herman Ruth
Calvert	Skipjack
Chesapeake Bay	Song
Civil War	Sport
Climate(s)	Star-Spangled Banner
Constitution	State House
Crop(s)	Terrapin
County (-ies)	Treaty of Paris
Frederick Douglass	Harriet Tubman
Dog / Cat	War of 1812
Executive Branch	Washington, DC
Fish (-ing)	White Oak

Additional Terms

Choose as many additional terms as you would like and write them in the squares. Repeat each as desired.
Cut out the squares and randomly distribute them to the class.
Instruct the students to place their square on the center space of their card.

Maryland Bingo

Clues for Additional Terms

Write three clues for each of your additional terms.

_____ 1. 2. 3.	_____ 1. 2. 3.
_____ 1. 2. 3.	_____ 1. 2. 3.
_____ 1. 2. 3.	_____ 1. 2. 3.

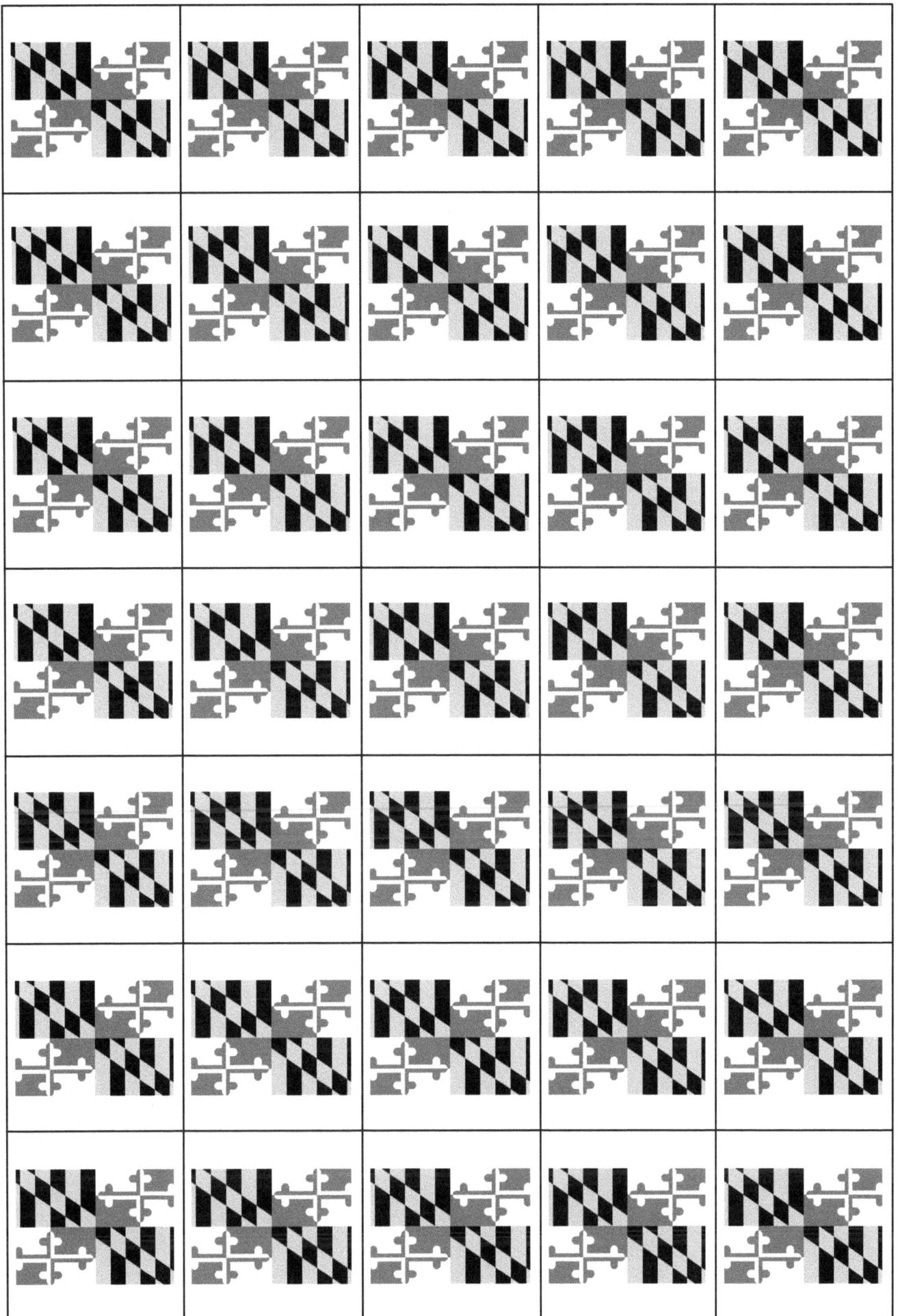

Annapolis 1. ___ is the capital of Maryland. It was the temporary capital of the United States after the signing of the Treaty of Paris in 1783. 2. The U.S. Naval Academy is located in ___.	**Antietam** 1. The Civil War battle known as the Battle of ___ was the nation's bloodiest one-day battle. 2. The Battle of ___ took place on September 17, 1862. After twelve hours of combat, about 23,000 soldiers were killed, wounded or missing.
Atlantic Coastal Plain 1. The ___ covers about half of the state's land area. It includes the entire Eastern Shore of the Chesapeake Bay and part of the Western Shore. Much of the Western Shore is good farmland. 2. The Delmarva Peninsula is in the ___. It is made up of sections of Maryland and Virginia and all of Delaware.	**Backbone Mountain** 1. ___ is is a ridge of the Allegheny Mountains. 2. Hoye-Crest is a summit on ___. At 3,360 feet, it is the highest point in the state.
Baltimore 1. ___ is the largest city in Maryland. 2. ___'s Inner Harbor is a historic seaport and a major tourist attraction.	**Baltimore Oriole** 1. The ___ is the state bird. 2. The male of this species has bright orange plumage.
Benjamin Banneker 1. This African-American mathematician and scientist was born in Maryland on November 9, 1731. 2. In 1791 ___ assisted in surveying the Federal District, which is now Washington, DC.	**Bethesda** 1. ___ is the home of the Walter Reed National Military Medical Center. 2. ___ is the home of the National Institutes of Health.
Black-Eyed Susan 1. The ___ is the official floral emblem of Maryland. 2. This flowering plant grows over three feet tall and has green leaves up to six inches long.	**Blue Crab(s)** 1. The ___ is the state crustacean. 2. The Chesapeake Bay is famous for its ___. The harvesting of ___ are of great economic importance to the state.
Maryland Bingo	© **Barbara M. Peller**

Blue Ridge 1. The ___ Region is west of the Piedmont. 2. In Maryland the ___ Region is represented by a narrow, mountainous section of land between the Piedmont and the Appalachian Ridge and Valley.	**Border States** 1. Slave states that did not secede before April 1861 are called ___. 2. Maryland was one of four ___ never to secede.
Border(s) 1. Maryland's land ___ include Delaware, Pennsylvania, Virginia, West Virginia, and Washington, DC. 2. These bodies of water ___ Maryland: Chesapeake Bay and the Atlantic Ocean.	**Cabinet** 1. The governor's executive council is known as the ___. 2. The governor's executive council, or ___, includes the heads of the 20 departments which oversee most state agencies.
Calvert 1. Riversdale, also known as the ___ Mansion, is a plantation home that was built between 1801 and 1807. It is a National Historic Landmark. 2. The title "Baron Baltimore" was held by several members of the ___ family.	**Chesapeake Bay** 1. ___ is the largest estuary in the United States. It was created more than 10,000 years ago when glaciers melted and flooded the Susquehanna River Valley. 2. ___ divides separates the Eastern Shore from the main part of the state.
Civil War 1. Maryland remained in the Union during the ___. 2. Maryland was a border state during the ___. Although it did not secede, many fought for the Confederacy.	**Climate(s)** 1. Maryland generally has a temperate ___. Despite its small size, however, the ___ in the state varies. 2. The differences in the ___ of the various regions is due partly to the differences in elevation and nearness to water.
Constitution 1. Maryland ratified the ___ of the United States on April 28, 1788. 2. Maryland was the 7th state to ratify the ___.	**Crop(s)** 1. Greenhouse and nursery products, corn, soybeans, wheat, hay, barley, tomatoes, apples and tobacco are important ___. 2. Most of the state's ___ income is from greenhouse and nursery products.
Maryland Bingo	

County (-ies)	Dog / Cat
1. There are 23 ___. Although a municipality, Baltimore City is often listed with the ___. 2. There are 3 forms of ___ government: ___ commissioners, code home rule, and charter home rule.	1. The Chesapeake Bay retriever is the official state ___. 2. The calico is the official state ___.

Frederick Douglass	Executive Branch
1. This abolitionist, orator, writer and statesman was born in a slave cabin in February 1818 near the town of Easton, Maryland. 2. His autobiography is entitled *Narrative of the Life of ___, an American Slave, Written by Himself.*	1. The governor is head of the ___. The present-day governor is [fill in]. 2. The governor, the lieutenant governor, the secretary of state, the attorney general and the state treasurer are all part of the ___.

Fish (-ing)	Flag
1. ___ is a major industry in the state. The Chesapeake Bay is known for its seafood production, especially blue crabs, clams and oysters. 2. The state ___ is the rockfish, or striped bass.	1. Maryland's state ___ is the only one based on British heraldry. 2. The design of the state ___ was based on the coat of arms adopted by George Calvert, the first Lord Baltimore.

Fossil(s)	Frederick
1. *Astrodon johnstoni* is the state dinosaur. ___ teeth from these giant sauropods were found in Maryland in 1858. 2. The *Ecphora gardnerae gardnerae is* an extinct snail. Its shell is the state ___.	1. ___ is the second largest city in the state. 2. Fort Detrick is located in ___.

Industry (-ies)	Judicial Branch
1. The manufacture of computer and electronic products is an important ___ . 2. Farming, coal mining, steel manufacturing, communications equipment, fishing, and government services are important ___.	1. The head of the ___ of state government is the Chief Judge of the Court of Appeals. 2. Four court divisions make up the ___: the Court of Appeals, the Court of Special Appeals, the Circuit Courts, and the District Court of Maryland.

Maryland Bingo

Legislative Branch 1. The General Assembly is the ___ of state government. 2. The General Assembly, or ___, comprises the Senate and the House of Delegates.	**Livestock** 1. Most of the state's farm income comes from ___. Broilers, or young chickens, are Maryland's leading ___ products. 2. Milk and other dairy products are also important ___ products.
Mid-Atlantic 1. ___ refers to the region of the United States generally located between New England and the South. 2. Maryland is in the ___ Region of the United States.	**Piedmont** 1. The ___ Region cuts across the state from the northeast through central Maryland. It is marked by low, rolling landscapes and fertile valleys. 2. Frederick Valley in the ___. Dairy farming is important in the valley.
Plateau 1. The ___ Region includes the western part of Allegany County and all of Garrett County, the westernmost county in Maryland. 2. Maryland's highest mountains are in the ___ Region.	**Province of Maryland** 1. The ___ was founded in 1632. Until 1695 St. Mary's City was the capital. 2. The ___ began as a proprietary colony of the English Lord Baltimore. It began as a haven for English Catholics.
Ridge and Valley 1. The ___ Region of Maryland is the northern strip of land that separates West Virginia from Pennsylvania. 2. The eastern part of the ___ Region is dominated by the Hagerstown Valley, which is part of the Great Appalachian Valley.	**River(s)** 1. Major ___ include the Patapsco, the Patuxent, and the Potomac. 2. Most ___ in the state run into the Chesapeake Bay.
George Herman Ruth 1. Better known as Babe, this baseball superstar was born in Baltimore. 2. ___ had several nicknames. One was "Sultan of Swat."	**Skipjack** 1. The ___ is a traditional fishing boat used on Chesapeake Bay for oyster dredging. 2. This sailboat remains in service due to laws restricting the use of powerboats in the state oyster fishery.
Maryland Bingo	© **Barbara M. Peller**

Song 1. The state ___ is "Maryland, My Maryland." 2. The first verse of the state ___ begins, "The despot's heel is on thy shore, Maryland!"	**Sport** 1. Jousting is the official state ___. Jousting tournaments have been held in Maryland since early colonial times. 2. Lacrosse is the official state team ___. The Lacrosse Museum and National Hall of Fame is in Baltimore.
Star-Spangled Banner 1. Its lyrics come from "[Defence] of Fort McHenry," a poem written by Francis Scott Key. 2. Francis Scott Key wrote the lyrics to this anthem after witnessing the bombardment of Fort McHenry during the War of 1812.	**State House** 1. The Maryland ___ supports the largest wooden dome in the country built without nails. 2. The Maryland ___ is the oldest capital building in current use. It was built in 1772.
Terrapin 1. The state reptile is the diamondback ___. 2. The diamondback ___ is the official mascot of the University of Maryland College Park.	**Treaty of Paris** 1. The ___ was signed in the Maryland State House. It put an end to the Revolutionary War. 2. The ___, signed on September 3, 1783, ended the American Revolutionary War.
Harriet Tubman 1. Her real name was Araminta Harriet Ross. She was born in 1820 in Dorchester County. 2. After escaping slavery, she helped many find their way to freedom via the Underground Railroad.	**War of 1812** 1. Although British forces seized and burned Washington during the ___, the assault on Baltimore did not succeed. 2. The British Navy bombarded Fort McHenry in Baltimore on September 13 and14 during the ___. They retreated the next day.
Washington, DC 1. Maryland and Virginia donated land to the federal government for the creation of the new national capital of ___. Virginia's portion was returned. 2. Maryland donated all the land that is now Washington, DC.	**White Oak** 1. The ___ is the state tree. 2. The most famous example of the ___ was at Wye Mills, in Talbot County; however, in 2002 it was felled during a thunderstorm.

Maryland Bingo

Maryland Bingo

River(s)	Annapolis	Atlantic Coastal Plain	Constitution	Baltimore
Civil War	Antietam	War of 1812	Livestock	Skipjack
Harriet Tubman	Legislative Branch		Piedmont	Washington, DC
Treaty of Paris	George Herman Ruth	Terrapin	Judicial Branch	Province of Maryland
Dog / Cat	Frederick Douglass	Cabinet	Star-Spangled Banner	Flag

Maryland Bingo: Card No. 1

Maryland Bingo

Treaty of Paris	Harriet Tubman	Fish (-ing)	Fossil(s)	Industry (-ies)
Province of Maryland	Calvert	Bethesda	George Herman Ruth	Mid-Atlantic
Blue Crab(s)	Frederick Douglass		Executive Branch	Terrapin
Sport	Ridge and Valley	Legislative Branch	White Oak	Baltimore
Skipjack	War of 1812	Cabinet	Civil War	Star-Spangled Banner

Maryland Bingo

Frederick Douglass	Terrapin	Calvert	Judicial Branch	Harriet Tubman
Sport	Antietam	Black-Eyed Susan	Annapolis	County (-ies)
George Herman Ruth	War of 1812		Mid-Atlantic	Backbone Mountain
Legislative Branch	Blue Crab(s)	Dog / Cat	Plateau	Fish (-ing)
Star-Spangled Banner	Blue Ridge	Cabinet	White Oak	Industry (-ies)

Maryland Bingo: Card No. 3

Maryland Bingo

Legislative Branch	Mid-Atlantic	Atlantic Coastal Plain	Blue Ridge	Industry (-ies)
Sport	Benjamin Banneker	Annapolis	Fossil(s)	Harriet Tubman
Piedmont	Calvert		Flag	Constitution
Terrapin	White Oak	War of 1812	Cabinet	Bethesda
Border States	Skipjack	Baltimore Oriole	Star-Spangled Banner	Washington, DC

Maryland Bingo: Card No. 4

Maryland Bingo

Skipjack	Baltimore	George Herman Ruth	Bethesda	Blue Ridge
Sport	Terrapin	Black-Eyed Susan	Executive Branch	Antietam
Atlantic Coastal Plain	Washington, DC		Livestock	Crop(s)
Flag	Industry (-ies)	River(s)	White Oak	Border(s)
Calvert	Cabinet	Harriet Tubman	Legislative Branch	Piedmont

Maryland Bingo: Card No. 5

© Barbara M. Peller

Maryland Bingo

Backbone Mountain	Mid-Atlantic	Fish (-ing)	Industry (-ies)	Washington, DC
Judicial Branch	George Herman Ruth	Border(s)	Annapolis	Harriet Tubman
Fossil(s)	Border States		Benjamin Banneker	Executive Branch
Cabinet	Dog / Cat	White Oak	Baltimore Oriole	Atlantic Coastal Plain
Province of Maryland	Bethesda	River(s)	Piedmont	Chesapeake Bay

Maryland Bingo

River(s)	Mid-Atlantic	Crop(s)	Terrapin	Calvert
Province of Maryland	Industry (-ies)	Frederick Douglass	Antietam	Plateau
Washington, DC	Constitution		Executive Branch	Benjamin Banneker
Legislative Branch	Sport	Black-Eyed Susan	Treaty of Paris	Blue Crab(s)
Cabinet	Blue Ridge	White Oak	Baltimore Oriole	Backbone Mountain

Maryland Bingo

Piedmont	Mid-Atlantic	Climate(s)	Judicial Branch	Benjamin Banneker
Plateau	Atlantic Coastal Plain	Fossil(s)	Washington, DC	Bethesda
Chesapeake Bay	Blue Ridge		Industry (-ies)	Baltimore
Star-Spangled Banner	Legislative Branch	Treaty of Paris	Border States	Sport
War of 1812	Cabinet	Baltimore Oriole	George Herman Ruth	Province of Maryland

Maryland Bingo: Card No. 8

Maryland Bingo

Executive Branch	Calvert	Frederick Douglass	Chesapeake Bay	Blue Ridge
Border States	Industry (-ies)	Piedmont	George Herman Ruth	Mid-Atlantic
County (-ies)	River(s)		Antietam	Climate(s)
Border(s)	Baltimore	Dog / Cat	Livestock	Crop(s)
Sport	White Oak	Black-Eyed Susan	Treaty of Paris	Flag

Maryland Bingo: Card No. 9

Maryland Bingo

Treaty of Paris	Judicial Branch	Benjamin Banneker	Fossil(s)	Chesapeake Bay
Washington, DC	Bethesda	Annapolis	Antietam	Industry (-ies)
Blue Ridge	Mid-Atlantic		Constitution	Blue Crab(s)
Dog / Cat	Flag	Border(s)	White Oak	County (-ies)
Black-Eyed Susan	Province of Maryland	Fish (-ing)	Skipjack	Piedmont

Maryland Bingo

Backbone Mountain	Mid-Atlantic	George Herman Ruth	Border(s)	Province of Maryland
Climate(s)	County (-ies)	Livestock	Executive Branch	Annapolis
Sport	Industry (-ies)		Fish (-ing)	Frederick Douglass
Black-Eyed Susan	Harriet Tubman	White Oak	Blue Ridge	Treaty of Paris
Border States	Cabinet	River(s)	Baltimore Oriole	Calvert

Maryland Bingo: Card No. 11

Maryland Bingo

Calvert	Baltimore	County (-ies)	Judicial Branch	Executive Branch
Frederick Douglass	Province of Maryland	Atlantic Coastal Plain	Baltimore Oriole	Antietam
River(s)	Crop(s)		Washington, DC	Fossil(s)
Cabinet	Plateau	Industry (-ies)	Treaty of Paris	Sport
Mid-Atlantic	Climate(s)	Blue Ridge	Border States	Bethesda

Maryland Bingo: Card No. 12

Maryland Bingo

Border(s)	Baltimore	Backbone Mountain	County (-ies)	Washington, DC
Atlantic Coastal Plain	Climate(s)	Industry (-ies)	Executive Branch	Blue Crab(s)
Judicial Branch	Bethesda		Frederick Douglass	Crop(s)
Piedmont	White Oak	Benjamin Banneker	Blue Ridge	Treaty of Paris
Cabinet	Flag	Baltimore Oriole	River(s)	Livestock

Maryland Bingo: Card No. 13

Maryland Bingo

Civil War	Industry (-ies)	George Herman Ruth	Executive Branch	Border States
Bethesda	River(s)	County (-ies)	Antietam	Mid-Atlantic
Border(s)	Constitution		Fish (-ing)	Black-Eyed Susan
Flag	White Oak	Blue Ridge	Benjamin Banneker	Backbone Mountain
Cabinet	Fossil(s)	Blue Crab(s)	Province of Maryland	Piedmont

Maryland Bingo: Card No. 14

Maryland Bingo

Livestock	Executive Branch	George Herman Ruth	Calvert	Judicial Branch
Backbone Mountain	Fish (-ing)	Annapolis	Atlantic Coastal Plain	Border States
Washington, DC	River(s)		Harriet Tubman	Mid-Atlantic
Cabinet	County (-ies)	Climate(s)	White Oak	Border(s)
Province of Maryland	Sport	Baltimore Oriole	Chesapeake Bay	Frederick Douglass

Maryland Bingo

Benjamin Banneker	County (-ies)	Climate(s)	Chesapeake Bay	Ridge and Valley
Fossil(s)	Blue Crab(s)	Crop(s)	Plateau	Constitution
Border(s)	Baltimore		Washington, DC	Frederick Douglass
Legislative Branch	Bethesda	Cabinet	Livestock	Treaty of Paris
Border States	State House	Baltimore Oriole	Sport	Mid-Atlantic

Maryland Bingo: Card No. 16

Maryland Bingo

Black-Eyed Susan	Song	Frederick	County (-ies)	Civil War
Livestock	Border States	White Oak	Constitution	Crop(s)
Executive Branch	Piedmont		State House	Climate(s)
Flag	Province of Maryland	Treaty of Paris	George Herman Ruth	Blue Crab(s)
Dog / Cat	Border(s)	Calvert	Judicial Branch	Baltimore

Maryland Bingo: Card No. 17

Maryland Bingo

Chesapeake Bay	Blue Ridge	Bethesda	Border(s)	Fossil(s)
Mid-Atlantic	Black-Eyed Susan	Dog / Cat	Washington, DC	Border States
Executive Branch	Blue Crab(s)		Frederick	Atlantic Coastal Plain
Baltimore	Annapolis	White Oak	Treaty of Paris	Fish (-ing)
State House	County (-ies)	George Herman Ruth	Song	Backbone Mountain

Maryland Bingo

Washington, DC	Backbone Mountain	County (-ies)	Climate(s)	Treaty of Paris
Livestock	Judicial Branch	Mid-Atlantic	Calvert	Constitution
Song	Blue Ridge		Antietam	Harriet Tubman
Fish (-ing)	State House	Dog / Cat	Plateau	Frederick
Atlantic Coastal Plain	Ridge and Valley	Province of Maryland	Piedmont	Baltimore Oriole

Maryland Bingo

Civil War	Song	Judicial Branch	County (-ies)	Baltimore Oriole
Bethesda	Frederick Douglass	Sport	Dog / Cat	Fossil(s)
Baltimore	Crop(s)		Legislative Branch	Annapolis
Skipjack	War of 1812	Star-Spangled Banner	Plateau	State House
Terrapin	Piedmont	Ridge and Valley	Treaty of Paris	Frederick

Maryland Bingo

Livestock	Backbone Mountain	Plateau	County (-ies)	Skipjack
Baltimore	Frederick	Benjamin Banneker	Climate(s)	River(s)
Blue Crab(s)	Province of Maryland		Song	George Herman Ruth
Dog / Cat	Calvert	State House	Flag	Piedmont
Legislative Branch	Ridge and Valley	Baltimore Oriole	Black-Eyed Susan	Washington, DC

Maryland Bingo

Chesapeake Bay	Fish (-ing)	Frederick	Atlantic Coastal Plain	Border(s)
Fossil(s)	Judicial Branch	Harriet Tubman	Climate(s)	Antietam
Bethesda	Constitution		River(s)	Crop(s)
State House	Flag	Plateau	Annapolis	River(s)
Ridge and Valley	Black-Eyed Susan	Song	Blue Crab(s)	Terrapin

Maryland Bingo

Benjamin Banneker	Song	Calvert	Atlantic Coastal Plain	Baltimore Oriole
Backbone Mountain	Civil War	Province of Maryland	Livestock	Annapolis
Fish (-ing)	Border(s)		Star-Spangled Banner	River(s)
Blue Crab(s)	Ridge and Valley	State House	Black-Eyed Susan	Plateau
Skipjack	War of 1812	Piedmont	Dog / Cat	Frederick

Maryland Bingo

Benjamin Banneker	Piedmont	Civil War	Song	Climate(s)
Frederick	Baltimore Oriole	Plateau	Fossil(s)	River(s)
Crop(s)	Chesapeake Bay		Border(s)	Blue Crab(s)
Skipjack	Star-Spangled Banner	State House	Black-Eyed Susan	Baltimore
Terrapin	Legislative Branch	Ridge and Valley	Judicial Branch	War of 1812

Maryland Bingo

Legislative Branch	Plateau	Song	George Herman Ruth	Frederick
Annapolis	Baltimore	Livestock	Benjamin Banneker	Antietam
Flag	Climate(s)		Star-Spangled Banner	State House
Harriet Tubman	Skipjack	War of 1812	Ridge and Valley	Constitution
Baltimore Oriole	Civil War	Bethesda	Border States	Terrapin

Maryland Bingo

Frederick	Song	Fish (-ing)	Fossil(s)	Chesapeake Bay
Dog / Cat	Judicial Branch	Climate(s)	Civil War	Benjamin Banneker
Flag	Star-Spangled Banner		Constitution	Legislative Branch
Black-Eyed Susan	Atlantic Coastal Plain	Skipjack	Ridge and Valley	State House
Crop(s)	Border States	George Herman Ruth	War of 1812	Terrapin

Maryland Bingo

Fish (-ing)	Bethesda	Song	Civil War	Frederick Douglass
Skipjack	Star-Spangled Banner	Livestock	State House	Antietam
White Oak	War of 1812		Ridge and Valley	Legislative Branch
Chesapeake Bay	Backbone Mountain	Plateau	Terrapin	Annapolis
Border States	Constitution	Frederick	Harriet Tubman	Crop(s)

Maryland Bingo: Card No. 27

Maryland Bingo

Fish (-ing)	Civil War	Harriet Tubman	Song	Benjamin Banneker
Frederick Douglass	Frederick	Star-Spangled Banner	Fossil(s)	Constitution
War of 1812	Blue Crab(s)		Crop(s)	Dog / Cat
Treaty of Paris	Chesapeake Bay	Plateau	Ridge and Valley	State House
Atlantic Coastal Plain	Executive Branch	Border States	Terrapin	Skipjack

Maryland Bingo

Frederick	Civil War	Chesapeake Bay	Livestock	Executive Branch
Sport	Dog / Cat	Sport	Crop(s)	Harriet Tubman
Flag	Star-Spangled Banner		Antietam	Song
Frederick Douglass	Skipjack	Industry (-ies)	Ridge and Valley	State House
Benjamin Banneker	Climate(s)	Terrapin	Backbone Mountain	War of 1812

Maryland Bingo

Blue Ridge	Song	Fossil(s)	Executive Branch	State House
Annapolis	Civil War	Fish (-ing)	Constitution	Antietam
Flag	Border(s)		Crop(s)	Plateau
Terrapin	Backbone Mountain	Atlantic Coastal Plain	Ridge and Valley	Star-Spangled Banner
Skipjack	Washington, DC	War of 1812	Frederick	Harriet Tubman

Maryland Bingo: Card No. 30

www.ingramcontent.com/pod-product-compliance
Lightning Source LLC
LaVergne TN
LVHW061338060426
835511LV00014B/1985